EMBRACING BIBLICAL LITERACY

Patrick T. Brown, M.Div, Ed.D

WESTBOW
P R E S S®
A DIVISION OF THOMAS NELSON
& ZONDERVAN

Scripture quotations taken from the New American Standard Bible® (NASB), Copyright © 1960, 1962, 1963, 1968, 1971, 1972, 1973, 1975, 1977, 1995 by The Lockman Foundation Used by permission. www.Lockman.org

WestBow Press books may be ordered through booksellers or by contacting:

WestBow Press
A Division of Thomas Nelson & Zondervan
1663 Liberty Drive
Bloomington, IN 47403
www.westbowpress.com
1 (866) 928-1240

ISBN: 978-1-9736-6017-0 (sc)
ISBN: 978-1-9736-6016-3 (e)

Print information available on the last page.

WestBow Press rev. date: 04/30/2019

Dedication

This book is dedicated to my family and my International Theological College family. Your undiminishing support is without comparison.

Contents

Introduction

The book that you are about to engage is the most influential and controversial library that the human race has ever embraced, despite the many feverish attempts to burn, ban, and blaspheme against it. The Bible is an incredible book of history that proves there is a God who created all things. Most importantly, the Bible is the Word of God. It contains the mind of God and His will for each of our lives.

It is indispensable, that Christian leaders, pastors, Sunday school teachers and laity understand the value of biblical literacy. The quantity of biblical literacy is not as impactful or valuable without proper quality of its knowledge.

We live in an age of material and technological abundance. Access to and use of the Bible has become ever more convenient. The Bible is now practically everywhere, thanks especially to the smartphone app. However, ironically enough, biblical understanding and its use has become shallower and less serious as biblical access has become more convenient and easier. We are living in a culture that needs to heed God's warning.

People across the span of this world wrestle with these questions, if the Bible is so clear, why do we have so many commentaries and journals and books and dictionaries, all of which by no means agree and some of which exist for the major purpose of disagreeing with all who have gone before? Mark D. Thompson wrote in his book, *A Clear and Present Word: The Clarity of Scripture*, "The clarity of Scripture is that quality of the biblical text that, as God's communicative act, ensures its meaning is accessible to all who come to it in faith".

In this pithy piece, I want to attempt to clarify the doctrine of the clarity of Scripture, show the value of Bible difficulties, and suggest a way forward in a world full of conflict over the Bible.

1

What is the Bible?

The Bible is a historical record of God's work to Israel, including many of the words of the ancient prophets and some of the words spoken by God when He started His work. The author of the Bible is God. It is a history book written by God-inspired human beings. It records the principles by which many of the ancient saints and prophets served God, as well as the apostles' experiences of serving Him in more recent times. Obtaining this knowledge can serve as a guide for people seeking the true way to live in the present age. One can find many ways of life that cannot be found in other books. Because they are all the ways of life given to generations of prophets and apostles through their experience of the Holy Spirit's work, and because much of this language is of great value to people and gives them necessary sustenance, it is a book that everyone is eager and ready to read. And because there are so many secrets hidden in the Bible, people regard it differently than they do any other writing by great spiritual men.

The Bible is a very priceless paragon. It's true, and it will always be true; it's accurate, and it will always be enough; it's unchanging, yet it is living and able to speak to each of us.

The Scope of the Bible

The Bible is One Book

1. One Common Theme – Christ
2. One Common Author – God
3. One Common Purpose – Redemption

Etymology of the term "Bible"

The word "Bible" originates from the Greek biblos, a book, a roll; a variant form of bublos, the Egyptian papyrus and the paper made from its fibrous coat.

The Revelation of God is the process by which God unveils Himself and His will to human messengers. The Bible is divinely inspired, according to 2 Timothy 3:16 and 2 Peter 1:20-21. In the words of the Latin "sola scriptura", the Word of God is final.

Illumination of God refers to the Holy Spirit's work as He enlightens the human mind with spiritual understanding in order that man may seize the revealed truth, according to John 14:26 and 1 Corinthians 2:14

Inspiration of the Bible references God's inbreathing into the chosen men through the Holy Spirit, enabling him by divine guidance to deliver or record God's revealed message.

In the Scriptural sense it means God breathing into His messenger.

The Exceptionality of the Bible

- The Bible is a library of 66 books written by 40 authors over a period of 1500 years.
- 39 Old Testament books: 5 books of the law. 12 historical, 5 poetical, 17 prophetic.
- 27 New Testament books: 4 Gospels, 1 historical (Acts), 21 epistles (letters), 1 prophetic (Revelation).
- Topics include religion, history, law, science, poetry, drama, biography, prophecy.
- Authors are from different walks of life, educated and uneducated, kings and peasants, public officials and farmers, teachers and physicians.
- Authors wrote in different places: wilderness (Moses), dungeon (Jeremiah), prison (Paul), island (John).
- The Bible was written in times of war and peace as well as in times of joy and sorrow and hope and despair.
- The Bible was written on 3 continents: Asia, Africa, Europe.
- The Bible was written in 3 languages: Hebrew, Aramaic, Greek.

The Canonicity of the Bible

A biblical canon or canon of scripture is a set of texts which a particular religious community regards as authoritative scripture. The English word "canon" comes from the Greek word, Κανόνα, meaning rule or measuring stick.

TaNaK (Hebrew: תנ״ך), or Tanakh, is an acronym for the Hebrew Bible consisting of the initial Hebrew letters (T - N - K) of each of the text's three major portions. Since the ancient Hebrew language had no clear vowels, subsequent vowel sounds were added to the consonants resulting in the word TaNaK.

The major portions of the Hebrew Bible are represented by these three letters:

1. Torah (תורה) meaning "Instruction" or "Law." Also called the Chumash חומש meaning: "The five"; "The five books of Moses." Also called the "Pentateuch." The Torah is often referred to as the law of the Jewish people.
2. Nevi'im (נביאים) meaning "Prophets." This term is associated with anything to do with the prophets.
3. Ketuvim (כתובים) meaning "Writings." This part of the Tanakh is further separated into different sections including a group of history books, wisdom books, poetry books and psalms.

Development of the Bible

A. Early church history – ta biblia referred to the Old Testament
B. Jerome (4th Century) – referred to the Scripture as the Bibliotheca Divina (the divine library)

C. 5th Century – usage of ta biblia was extended to include the New Testament.

D. Somehow the neutral plural passed into the western languages as a feminine singular, so that the books became "The Book"
    English & French: Bible
    German: Bibel
    Spanish: Biblia
    Italian: Bibbia

E. First occurrences in English are in the 14th century – Chaucer and Wycliffe

F. The King James translation was published in 1611.

G. According to Wycliffe Global Alliance, in 2018, the complete Bible has been translated into 683 languages and the New Testament has been translated into 1534 languages. There are over 1750 versions of the Bible available on Bible.com, in over 1200 languages.

Notes

2

The Chronos and Organization of the Bible

The Old Testament has been divided into 4 divisions: Law, History, Poetry and Prophecy.

The Books of Law

There are five books of law in the Old Testament. The names of these books are Genesis, Exodus, Leviticus, Numbers and Deuteronomy. These books record the creation of man and the world by God and the early history of man. They tell how God raised up the nation of Israel as a people through which He could reveal Himself to the nations of the world.

These books record the laws of God. The best-known parts are the Ten Commandments (Exodus 20:3-17), the greatest of all commandments (Deuteronomy 6:5), and the second greatest commandment (Leviticus 19:18).

The Books of History

There are 12 books of history in the Old Testament. The names of the books of history are Joshua, Judges, Ruth, I and II Samuel I and II Kings, I and II Chronicles, Ezra, Nehemiah and Esther.

Locate these books in your Bible. They are found right after the books of law. The books of history cover a thousand-year history of God's people, Israel. Naturally they do not tell everything that happened, but they record the major events and show the results of both following and ignoring God's law.

The Books of Poetry

There are five books of poetry in the Old Testament. The names of the books of poetry are: Job, Psalms, Proverbs, Ecclesiastes and Song of Solomon. These books are the worship books of God's people, Israel. They still are used in worship by believers today.

The Books of Prophecy

The books of prophecy of the Old Testament are divided into two groups which are called Major and Minor prophetical books. This does not mean the Major Prophets are more important than the Minor Prophets. The title is simply used because the Major Prophets are longer books than the Minor Prophets. There are 17 books of prophecy in the Old Testament. The names of the books of the Major Prophets are Isaiah, Jeremiah, Lamentations, Ezekiel and Daniel. The names of the books by the Minor Prophets are Hosea, Nahum, Joel, Habakkuk, Amos, Zephaniah, Obadiah, Haggai, Jonah, Zechariah, Micah and Malachi.

These books are prophetic messages from God to His people about future events. Many of the prophecies have already been fulfilled, but some remain to be fulfilled in the future. Find these prophetic books in your Bible. They are the last books in the Old Testament.

New Testament Divisions

The New Testament has also been divided into four groups: Gospels, History, Letters, and Prophecy.

The Gospels

There are four books in the Gospels. The names of these books are: Matthew, Mark, Luke and John. These books tell about the life, death, and resurrection of Jesus. Their purpose is to lead you to believe that He is the Christ, the Son of God. Find the Gospels in your Bible and then read John 20:31 which states this purpose.

The Book of History

There is one book of history in the New Testament, the book of Acts. This book tells how the church began and fulfilled Christ's commission to spread the Gospel throughout the world. Locate this book in your Bible.

Letters

The letters are addressed to all believers. Their purpose is to guide them in living and help them do what Jesus commanded. Romans 12 is a good example of their teaching. The letters are also sometimes called "epistles" which means letters.

There are 21 letters in the New Testament. The names of these letters are: Romans, I and II Corinthians, Galatians, Ephesians, Philippians, Colossians, I and II Thessalonians, I and II Timothy, Titus, Philemon, Hebrews and James, I and II Peter, I, II and III John, Jude.

Prophecy

Revelation is the only book of prophecy in the New Testament. It tells of the final victory of Jesus and His people. Its purpose is to encourage you to keep living as a Christian should live until the end of time. Its message is summarized in Revelation 2:10.

Notes

3

Effective Bible Translations

Bible scholars often use the term "transliteration", but I've come realize that it is a foreign concept for many. I think it would be immensely purposeful to give definitive clarity for you today. The term "translation" is quite a familiar concept. A translator takes a text in one language and converts it to the equivalent text in another language. In the case of biblical translation, a translator takes the ancient Greek, Hebrew, and Aramaic text, which is unreadable to most Christians, and converts it to the equivalent text in English (or the common tongue for another culture).

The problem with translation is that there is not always equivalent text from one language to another. We don't just have different words; we have different sentence structures, different figures of speech, and some words which have no match in a different language, or which carry different connotations and nuances. God did a very good job when he confused the language at Babel, and languages have only grown more complex and confusing since then. Sometimes these difficulties can be solved by paraphrasing the text.

Other times translators will use a similar term and then expand the text to include a definition within it. But in many cases, when translators come across a word with no exact English equivalent, they will just skip translating that word entirely. This is a transliteration. A translator takes a word in one language, adjusts it a little to make it look and sound more like another language, and then places it in with the rest of the text in that other language. In biblical translation, a translator would take, for example, a Greek word and adjust it to fit in in our character set, usually changing the pronunciation a bit to make it sound more like English. (Strictly speaking, what I describe here is known as partial transliteration. For our purposes, just calling it a transliteration should suffice.)

This can be a very useful tool for translators, especially biblical translators who want to be careful not to make the translation seem like it means something the original does not. Better to just stick with the original than to give a faulty translation, right? But it can also cause other problems. A transliterated word essentially creates a new English word. And over time, these new words take on connotations and nuances of their own, which may not have been present in the original word they represent.

Examples

The best way to see how all this works is with an example. *Angel* is a transliterated word. It comes from the Greek word *aggelos*, which literally means "messenger" or "envoy." When we hear the word *angel*, we usually think of a heavenly being with wings, but such a meaning is not actually present in *aggelos*. However, in many examples, these messengers were indeed beings sent from heaven. In some cases, the biblical authors were referring to these beings when they used *aggelos*, while in other cases they just meant normal human messengers.

We could draw a parallel with the word *alien*. An alien is just a foreigner. However, the word has gained an extra connotation so that it is often used to mean a foreign being from outer space. Yet we still sometimes use it to refer to human foreigners. In like manner, the New Testament authors went back and forth between using *aggelos* for heavenly beings or for human messengers. Many English translations try to reflect this by going back and forth between the transliteration and the translation respectively, yet this can be problematic as well, as sometimes the true meaning is ambiguous. Take, for example, "the angels of the seven churches" (Revelation 1:20). Were these heavenly beings assigned to those churches? Or were they the human messengers for the churches? I would tend to think the latter, yet the most common translations transliterate that word here.

It is good to know when you are looking at a transliteration, and it is good to know the literal meaning of that transliteration. Sometimes this can make a world of difference in understanding an otherwise confusing verse.

The following are just a few more examples of transliterated words in the New Testament:

- *Apostle* comes from *apostlos* and means "one who is sent."
- *Baptism* comes from *baptisma* and means "immersion."

- *Christ* comes from *cristos* and means "anointed one."
- *Deacon* comes from *diakonos* and means "servant."
- *Epistle* comes from *epistole* and means "letter."

Should I continue through the whole alphabet? For now, just be on the lookout for other transliterated words. Remember that the connotations they have today may be very different from what the original represented.

Hebrew, Greek and Aramaic are the ONLY languages that God chose to communicate His inspired Word. The orthodox doctrine of the inspiration of Scripture has always been restricted to the original Hebrew and Greek manuscripts as penned by the biblical writers (or their scribes), not to copies or translations of these documents. Reading the original biblical languages is like hearing the voice in person, as opposed listening through a distorted, cracking and hissing AM radio station.

The single, most important, starting point for biblical exegesis is grammar. Our primary concern must be with the grammar of the original language, not the English translation, and for this we need to know the original biblical language. A text simply CANNOT mean what the grammar of that text does not support.

Knowing biblical Hebrew and biblical Greek unveils the interpretive options of a given text—and assists in properly adjudicating among them. In the Greek language the genitive case alone has over thirty different grammatical functions, of which translators must choose only one in any given occurrence; English readers frequently have little clue what possibilities the translators rejected.

Knowing Biblical Hebrew and Greek gives the

interpreter useable access to invaluable exegetical tools. Certain passages of Scripture have multiple possibilities for meaning. Some translations footnote (usually one of) the grammatical options, but many do not. When, say the King James Version differs from the New International Version, how will you determine which of them gives the best interpretation? "Gut feeling?" "Holy Spirit Guidance?" For this, readers need a knowledge of the biblical languages and access to grammars, lexica, and scholarly commentaries that deal directly with the original text, little of which will make any sense to those unschooled in biblical languages.

Reading the text in the original biblical languages develops and reinforces a careful, detailed hermeneutical approach. Having to establish the precise use of a case, mood or voice forces the interpreter to consider all the various possibilities of meaning inherent in the language of the text. When it comes to hermeneutics, (biblical interpretation), attention to detail often brings a huge exegetical (understanding) dividend from this investment.

Reading the biblical text in the original Hebrew or Greek languages also identifies the authors' emphases. Here we think specifically of rhetorical features, such as alliteration, assonance, poetic structure, chiasm, marked/ unmarked word order, and the like, most of which are completely lost in translation—but all of which are clearly discernable to those schooled in the biblical languages.

Learning the biblical languages is a crucial antidote to hermeneutical arrogance. Grappling with texts in their original biblical language repeatedly calls our preconceived notions about the meaning of these texts to account; it checks unfounded certainty and preformed conclusions.

Congregations naturally put their trust (often, sad to say, blind trust) in their spiritual leaders—and sometimes for very laudable reasons. But this does not obviate the danger of such a practice, and it certainly makes preachers and teachers of God's Word even more responsible for "cutting a smooth path for the Word of Truth" as Paul says in 2 Timothy 2:15.

Notes

4

The Problem of
Biblical Illiteracy

In my opinion, many people are deeply religious and at the same time, profoundly ignorant about religion and the Bible. The U.S. Religious Knowledge Survey has shown that America is among the most religious of the world's developed nations. Nearly sixty percent of adults said religion is "very important" in their lives, and about forty percent indicated they attend worship services at least once a week. However, it also showed that large numbers of Americans are uninformed about the tenets, practices, history and leading figures of major faith traditions including their own. Ironically, Mormons (often considered a cult by evangelical Christians) obtained the highest score, sixty-six percent, on questions regarding Christianity and Bible knowledge compared to fifty percent for Protestants and forty-five percent for Catholics.

It gets worse! Only sixty-three percent of those surveyed correctly identified Genesis as the first book of the Bible.

An alarming fifty-three percent of Protestants could not correctly identify the four gospels of the Bible or Martin Luther as the person whose writings and actions inspired the Protestant Reformation. Forty-five percent of Catholics did not know their church teaches transubstantiation, especially in the Roman Catholic Church, the conversion of the Eucharist elements into the body and blood of Christ.

Biblical Illiteracy Defined

The irony is that although sixty-five percent of Americans agree that the Bible answers all the basic questions of life, twenty-eight percent of Americans rarely or have never read the Bible. Illiteracy is generally defined as the inability to read and write, but biblical illiteracy is generally described as a lack of familiarity with the Bible, rather than a lack of ability to read it. In other words, "Bible" illiteracy is not the unfortunate, unintentional inability to read and understand Scripture; it is the unfortunate, intentional neglect of the Scripture.

How Did We Reach this Point?

So how is it that we find ourselves in the middle of a spiritual famine?

1. Diversion

Every time I teach a class relative to biblical interpretation and spiritual growth and development, I ask students why is it that so few people in this generation are zealous about the things of God. I can't remember a time when I've asked that question and someone hasn't mentioned diversion. Social networking, texting, face book, television, video games and places dedicated to amusement ("amusement" parks, for example) pull our attention away from God's Word. These fun and interesting activities occupy time that we could spend reading, studying and memorizing the Bible and they divert our thoughts during times we could spend meditating on God's Word throughout the day. When we walk from one meeting to another, are our thoughts naturally moving to Scripture and prayer? As we leave a college class, are we thinking on the things of God that we have learned from the Bible? Or do we immediately check to see whether someone has direct messaged us?

In 1986, Neil Postman published an influential cultural essay titled "Amusing Ourselves to Death." He argued that personal freedoms would disappear not when a totalitarian government-imposed oppression from the outside (like George Orwell pictured in his book 1984), but rather when people came "to love their oppression, to adore the technologies that undo their capacities to think. We shouldn't assume that these distractions have no effect on our perceptions of God.

2. Priorities

Priorities are not as simple as "God first, family second and church third." What does that expression mean anyway? Every time I must choose between reading my Bible and spending time with my family, should I read my Bible? No. Priorities aren't based upon a simple hierarchy; they require equal balance of activities in relationship to one another. But it is a fitting question to ask: For a person who is working full time, what is the appropriate quantity of time that should be spent (on average) with one's spouse or children, in house or yard work, exercising and resting? How much time should you devote to building relationships with unbelieving neighbors or serving in your church? Let's grant for the sake of discussion that the exact balance of priorities will vary somewhat from person to person. Does this mean that we can weight our priorities any way we want? Absolutely not. "Meditating day and night" on God's Word is something that everyone must do. It is basic to the Christian life. It seems to me, then, that in any weighting of priorities the following scenarios are out of bounds:

- More time watching television than reading, studying, or memorizing God's Word
- More time on social networking sites than reading God's Word
- More time playing video games than reading God's Word

Almost everyone I know spends more time on one of these activities than they do reading, studying and memorizing the Bible. Shall we call this anything other than what it is? We don't like to talk about sin, but this is sin. James says, "[17] Therefore, to one who knows *the* [a] right thing to do and does not do it, to him it is sin." (James 4:17). We need a revival of the Bible. And many of us need to repent of our misplaced priorities.

3. Overconfidence

Of all the diverse comments I have heard from Christians over the years, the one that disturbs me perhaps more than any other is, "We already know more of the Bible than we put into practice anyway." This comment betrays far more about the speaker than it does about reality. First, it demonstrates that the one who said it isn't trying very hard to learn the Bible. Second, it reveals that the speaker is passive about applying it. And third, it confirms that the speaker assumes everyone shares the same passive attitude about the Bible. To what end? Should we stop studying the Bible until we have perfectly put into practice what we already know? The assumptions behind this statement are not only misplaced; they are patently false. We don't know enough about the Bible, we aren't putting enough effort into learning it, and everyone doesn't agree about this.

My sense is that comments like these are most often made by people who have grown up in the church but who have never personally committed themselves to learning the Word. So, let's get honest for a moment. How many of us who grew up in the church learned more than a few disconnected Bible stories simply because we attended Sunday schools and youth groups? Unless we decided at some point to begin to read and learn the Bible on our own, we never even learned how to find anything in the Bible, not even the stories. (Example: In what book of the Bible is the story of King Saul whom we mentioned earlier? Answer: 1 Samuel.) We learned precious little about biblical theology. (Example: How are the Old Testament sacrifices related to the coming of Christ?) We didn't learn why we believe what we claim to believe.

Notes

5

Biblical Literacy

Biblical literacy occurs when a person, with access to a Bible in a language he or she understands, consistently reads or hears the truth of the Word of God with personal understanding. A Gallup poll showed a decline in Bible reading among Americans from seventy-three percent in the 1980s to fifty-nine percent in 2000. The dismal statistics related to the frequency of Bible reading are summarized as follows:

16% read every day
21% read weekly
12% read monthly
10% less than monthly
41% rarely or never read the Bible

There are three unique qualities that make the Bible different from any other book.

1. The Bible's unity
2. Fulfilled prophecies
3. Personal experiences

First, the Bible is one unified book which was written in a span of 1600 years through 40 authors, 3 continents and 3 languages and still managed to have a uniformity throughout its accounts.

Second, the Bible documents many fulfilled prophecies. There were 333 prophecies of Christ mentioned hundreds of years before He ever came to earth. 150 of them occurred in the 6 hours he hung on the cross. History, Science and Geography confirms it. Scientists of the day believed that the Earth was flat while the Bible said it was round (Isaiah 40:22). Noah's Ark, the walls of Jericho, and Jesus' tomb were all found.

And finally, many people acclaim the Bible's impact on their personal experiences. They attribute their reading, studying and believing Scripture to changes in their lives. The Bible brings success and victory. The Scripture refers to itself as: a light that reveals and directs (Psalm 119:105), water that cleanses (Ephesians 5:25-27), a seed that brings fruitfulness (Luke 8:4-15), a fire that purges (Jeremiah 23:29), a hammer that breaks and honey that heals (Psalm 19:7-11).

Read it. For serious readers it takes 72 hours to read the whole Bible. Most people watch 33 hours of TV a week and 14 hours on social media per week. Think about it if you read 15 minutes a day and practice discipline you could read the Bible in one year. Listen to it. Faith comes by hearing and hearing from the Word of God. If you're someone who does not like to read at all then start with listening to the Bible.

Memorize it. Storing God's Word in your mind will allow the Holy Spirit to bring it up during a temptation or trial. Start with some of the most known Scriptures, review them, read them, recite them and repeat. If you repeat a verse by memory once a day for 100 days it will be in your permanent long-term memory. During temptation you can be like Jesus who will say to the devil, "It is written". Memorizing the Scripture like this will help you to conquer sin (Psalm 119:11).

Meditate on it. God told Joshua to meditate in His Word day and night. Meditation means to contemplate on something. Biblical meditation stands in contrast to many forms of meditation, which seeks to empty one's mind of rational thought. Biblical meditation seeks to fill your mind with truth.

Notes

6

Understanding Biblical Interpretation

There are several ways we can read and study the Bible, but one of the most effective and simple approaches to reading and understanding the Bible must be interpreting literally or figuratively.

Interpreting God's Word involves three basic steps:

Step 1: Surveillance —What does the text say?
Step 2: Interpretation—What does the text mean?
Step 3: Application— What the text says and means to me?

Step 1: Surveillance

Surveillance is the first and most important step in how to study the Bible. As you read the Bible text, you need to look carefully at what is said, and how it is said. Look for:

1. Terms, not words. Words can have many meanings, but terms are words used in a specific way in a specific context. (For instance, the word trunk could apply to a tree, a car, or a storage box. However, when you read, "That tree has a very large trunk," you know exactly what the word means, which makes it a term.)

2. Structure. If you look at your Bible, you will see that the text has units called paragraphs (indented or marked). A paragraph is a complete unit of thought. You can discover the content of the author's message by noting and understanding each paragraph unit.

3. Emphasis. The amount of space or the number of chapters or verses devoted to a specific topic will reveal the importance of that topic (for example, note the emphasis of Romans 9 and Psalms 119).

4. Repetition. This is another way an author demonstrates that something is important. One reading of 1 Corinthians 13, where the author uses the word "love" nine times in only 13 verses, communicates to us that love is the focal point of these 13 verses.

5. Relationships between ideas. Pay close attention, for example, to certain relationships that appear in the text.

6. Cause-and-effect: "His master said to him, 'Well done, good and faithful slave. You were faithful with a few things, I will put you in charge of many things; enter into the joy of your master." (Matthew 25:21).

7. Ifs and thens: "and My people [a]who are called by My name humble themselves and pray and seek My face and turn from their wicked ways, then I will hear from heaven, will forgive their sin and will heal their land." (2 Chronicles 7:14).

8. Questions and answers: "Who is the King of glory? The Lord strong and mighty, The Lord mighty in battle." (Psalm 24:8).

9. Comparisons and contrasts. "You have heard that [a]the ancients were told, 'You shall not commit murder' and 'Whoever commits murder shall be [b] liable to the court. " (Matthew 5:21).

10. Literary form. The Bible is literature, and the three main types of literature in the Bible are discourse (the epistles), prose (Old Testament history), and poetry (the Psalms). Considering the type of literature makes a great deal of difference when you read and interpret the Scriptures.

11. Atmosphere. The author had a particular reason or burden for writing each passage, chapter, and book. Be sure you notice the mood or tone or urgency of the writing.

After you have considered these things, you then are ready to ask the "Wh" questions: **Who? What? Where? When?** Who are the people in this passage? What is happening in this passage? Where is this story taking place? When in time (of day, of the year, in history) is it? Asking these four "Wh" questions can help you notice terms and identify atmosphere.

An example of theses interrogatives can be found as we consider Psalm 34:1:

Who- I
What- Will Bless
Whom- The lord
When- At all times
Where- His praise shall continually be in my mouth

The answers will also enable you to use your imagination to recreate the scene you're reading about. As you answer the "Wh" questions and imagine the event, you'll probably come up with some questions of your own. Asking those additional questions for understanding will help to build a bridge between observation (the first step) and interpretation (the second step) of the Bible study process.

Step 2: Interpretation

Interpretation is discovering the meaning of a passage, the author's main thought or idea. Answering the questions that arise during observation will help you in the process of interpretation.

Five clues (called "the five C's") can help you determine the author's main point(s):

1. Context. You can answer seventy-five percent of your questions about a passage when you read the text. Reading the text involves looking at the near context (the verse immediately before and after) as well as the far context (the paragraph or the

chapter that precedes and/or follows the passage you're studying).

2. Cross-references. Let Scripture interpret Scripture. That is, let other passages in the Bible shed light on the passage you are looking at. At the same time, be careful not to assume that the same word or phrase in two different passages means the same thing.

3. Culture. The Bible was written long ago, so when we interpret it, we need to understand it from the writers' cultural context.

4. Conclusion. Having answered your questions for understanding by means of context, cross-reference, and culture, you can make a preliminary statement of the passage's meaning. Remember that if your passage consists of more than one paragraph, the author may be presenting more than one thought or idea.

5. Consultation. Reading books known as commentaries, which are written by Bible scholars, can help you interpret Scripture.

Step 3: Application

Application is why we study the Bible. We want our lives to change; we want to be obedient to God and to grow more like Jesus Christ. After we have observed a passage and interpreted or understood it to the best of our ability, we must then apply its truth to our own life.

You'll want to ask the following questions of every passage of Scripture you study:

1. How does the truth revealed here affect my relationship with God?
2. How does this truth affect my relationship with others?
3. How does this truth affect me?
4. How does this truth affect my response to the enemy, Satan?

The application step is not completed by simply answering these questions; the key is putting into practice what God has taught you in your study. Although at any given moment you cannot be consciously applying everything you're learning through Bible study, you can be consciously applying something. And when you work on applying a truth to your life, God will bless your efforts by, as noted earlier, conforming you to the image of Jesus Christ.

Notes

7

Can We Understand
the Bible?

Biblical illiteracy is the result of being indifferent or outright hostile toward the Word of God. It is not only a problem in the world around us. Biblical illiteracy is also a serious problem within God's church. Until we solve the problem of biblical illiteracy in our own lives it will be impossible to reach the lost. We simply cannot teach what we don't know. Since we have talked about the importance of reading our Bibles, I want to spend some time in this lesson answering the question "Can We Understand the Bible."

We all believe the Bible is the inspired Word of God. However, simply believing the Bible is the Word of God does little good unless we take time to read the Bible. Therefore, finding some quiet time every day to immerse ourselves in the Word of God is the first step toward wiping out biblical illiteracy. But, simply reading the Bible has no lasting benefit unless we understand what we are reading.

The Bible was not written for entertainment or for the

pure joy of learning about biblical history. God intended for us to understand what we are reading, and then make application of those truths to our lives. The reason why this is so important is because understanding the Bible will not only help us live holy, godly lives here, but will also help us lead others to a belief and understanding of God's Word. Unfortunately, the world is filled with those who admire and revere the Bible, but they believe no one can really understand the Bible. They point to all the different churches with all their different beliefs and practices and say, "There is your proof that no one can really understand the Bible!" Unfortunately, even some of our own brethren have come to believe this lie. Some believe it's impossible to reach agreement on all the different doctrinal teachings in the Scriptures. Their way of handling doctrinal differences is to simply say, "Let's just agree to disagree." Agreeing to disagree is not how we achieve unity. I prefer to disagree to agree to disagree! So, I want us to spend some time addressing this misconception about God's divinely inspired Word.

1. We'll start by showing the Bible can and must be understood.
2. Then we'll look at steps we can take to understand the Scriptures, as well as traps to avoid that lead to misunderstanding or misapplying the Word of God.

Those who believe the Bible cannot be understood may be surprised to discover that the Bible says just the opposite. The Old Testament was written so that it could be understood. Jesus expected people in His day to understand the Old Testament Scriptures. He repeatedly challenged the false teachings of the religious leaders of His day by asking: "Have you not read?"

When Jesus and His disciples were accused of breaking the Sabbath laws, Jesus replied:

> "3But He said to them, "Have you not read what David did when he became hungry, he and his companions, 4 how he entered the house of God, and they ate the [a] consecrated bread, which was not lawful for him to eat nor for those with him, but for the priests alone? 5 Or have you not read in the Law, that on the Sabbath the priests in the temple [b]break the Sabbath and are innocent? 6 But I say to you that something greater than the temple is here. 7 But if you had known what this [c]means, 'I desire [d]compassion, and not a sacrifice,' you would not have condemned the innocent."
> (Matthew 12:3-8)

When these same religious leaders (Pharisees) tried to entrap Jesus on the question of divorce, Jesus replied:

> "4 And He answered and said, "Have you not read that He who created them from the beginning made them male and female, 5 and said, 'For this reason a man shall leave his father and mother and be joined to his wife, and the two shall become one flesh'? 6 So they are no longer two, but one flesh.

What therefore God has joined together, let
no man separate." (Matthew 19:4-6)

When the Sadducees tried to snare Jesus over the
question of the resurrection – something they denied –
Jesus replied:

> "[31] But regarding the resurrection of the
> dead, have you not read what was spoken to
> you by God: [32] 'I am the God of Abraham,
> and the God of Isaac, and the God of
> Jacob'? He is not the God of the dead but
> of the living." (Matthew 22:31-32)

The apostle Paul also appealed to the Old Testament
Scriptures on many occasions:
In Paul's efforts to prove Jesus was the Christ, we read:

> [2]And according to Paul's custom, he went
> to them, and for three Sabbaths reasoned
> with them from the Scriptures, [3] [a]
> explaining and [b]giving evidence that the
> [c]Christ had to suffer and rise again from
> the dead, and saying, "This Jesus whom I
> am proclaiming to you is the [d]Christ."
> (Acts 17:2-3)

In warning the Corinthians how God punished the
rebellious Israelites, Paul wrote:

> [6] Now these things happened as examples
> for us, so that we would not crave evil things

as they also craved. [7] Do not be idolaters, as some of them were; as it is written, "The people sat down to eat and drink, and stood up to play." ". . . [11] Now these things happened to them as an example, and they were written for our instruction, upon whom the ends of the ages have come. (1 Corinthians 10:6-7, 11)

Paul wrote the same thing to the church at Rome: [4] For whatever was written in earlier times was written for our instruction, so that through perseverance and the encouragement of the Scriptures we might have hope. (Romans 15:4)

Paul also reminded Timothy of the importance of the Old Testament Scriptures:

You, however, continue in the things you have learned and become convinced of, knowing from whom you have learned them, [15] and that from childhood you have known the sacred writings which are able to give you the wisdom that leads to salvation through faith which is in Christ Jesus. (2 Timothy 3:14-15)

Were there times when people needed help understanding the Old Testament Scriptures? Absolutely! Jesus helped His disciples understand how the Old Testament Scriptures were fulfilled in Him:

"[27] Then beginning [a]with Moses and [b] with all the prophets, He explained to them the things concerning Himself in all the Scriptures." (Luke 24:27)

"[30] Philip ran up and heard him reading Isaiah the prophet, and said, "Do you understand what you are reading?" [31] And he said, "Well, how could I, unless someone guides me?" And he invited Philip to come up and sit with him. [32] Now the passage of Scripture which he was reading was this:

"He was led as a sheep to slaughter;

And as a lamb before its shearer is silent,

So He does not open His mouth.

[33] "In humiliation His judgment was taken away; Who will [a]relate His [b]generation?

For His life is removed from the earth."

[34] The eunuch answered Philip and said, "Please tell me, of whom does the prophet say this? Of himself or of someone else?" [35] Then Philip opened his mouth, and beginning from this Scripture he preached Jesus to him. (Acts 8:30-35)

Why did these need help understanding of the Old Testament Scriptures? The Old Testament prophecies pointing to Christ and His spiritual kingdom were still cloaked in mystery in the early days of the church. However, when people were shown how those Scriptures were fulfilled in Jesus Christ, the mystery became clear.

What about the New Testament? Can we understand those writings? The writers of the New Testament Scriptures expected their readers to understand the things they wrote.

Writing Theophilus, Luke said:

> "[3] it seemed fitting for me as well, having [a]investigated everything carefully from the beginning, to write it out for you in consecutive order, most excellent Theophilus; [4] so that you may know the exact truth about the things you have been [b]taught." (Luke 1:3-4)

John said he wrote his gospel for the same reason:

> "[30] Therefore many other [a]signs Jesus also performed in the presence of the disciples, which are not written in this book; [31] but these have been written so that you may believe that Jesus is [b]the Christ, the Son of God; and that believing you may have life in His name." (John 20:30-31)

The apostle Paul certainly expected his readers to understand the things he wrote:

"¹³ For we write nothing else to you than what you read and understand, and I hope you will understand until the end; ¹⁴ just as you also partially did understand us, that we are your reason to be proud as you also are ours, in the day of our Lord Jesus." (2 Corinthians 1:13-14)

Even though the New Testament Scriptures were written to be understood, some of Paul's writings required diligent study to fully grasp the deep meaning.

Speaking of Apostle Paul's letters, Peter wrote:

"¹⁵ and regard the patience of our Lord as salvation; just as also our beloved brother Paul, according to the wisdom given him, wrote to you, ¹⁶ as also in all his letters, speaking in them of these things, in which are some things hard to understand, which the untaught and unstable distort, as they do also the rest of the Scriptures, to their own destruction." (2 Peter 3:15-16)

Even though some Scriptures may be "hard to understand" they are not impossible to understand. According to Peter, those who misunderstand the Scriptures are "untaught and unstable." Therefore, when "untaught and unstable" people teach, they frequently twist and pervert the Scriptures. So, let there be no mistake about it. The Bible, both the Old and New Testaments, was written to be understood. And since God did His part in giving us a Bible that could be understood, it's now up to us to do our part and learn what it says. God's expectations about learning and understanding His Word are found throughout the Scriptures.

Here are some things God expects us to do with the Word:

1. As new Christians we're told to desire it so we can grow spiritually:

   "[2] like newborn babies, long for the [a]pure [b]milk of the word, so that by it you may grow [c]in respect to salvation, (1 Peter 2:2)

2. God also expects us to continue growing:

   "[18] but grow in the grace and knowledge of our Lord and Savior Jesus Christ. To Him *be* the glory, both now and to the day of eternity. Amen." (2 Peter 3:18)

3. We are expected to increase in knowledge – in our understanding:

   "[10] so that you will walk in a manner worthy of the Lord, [a]to please *Him* in all respects, bearing fruit in every good work and [b] increasing in the [c]knowledge of God;" (Colossians 1:10)

We are also expected to reach a level of spiritual maturity where we can handle the "solid food" of the Word:

"[12] For though [a]by this time you ought to be teachers, you have need again for someone to teach you the [b]elementary principles of the oracles of God, and you have come to need milk and not solid food. [13] For everyone who partakes only of milk is not accustomed to the word of righteousness, for he is an infant. [14] But solid food is for the mature, who because of practice have their senses trained to discern good and evil." (Hebrews 5:12-14)

All this shows that the New Testament was also written to be understood – not all at once, but rather to be understood in stages. When we first come to Christ in obedience to the gospel, we learn to feed on the "milk" of the Word – simple, basis, first principles. But as we grow and mature spiritually, we are expected to be capable of digesting the "solid food" of the Word – the deeper, more complex principles taught in the Word, and how those principles should be applied.

That means, there is "milk" suitable to help mature the new Christian, and there is "solid food" to help the spiritually mature to continue remaining strong and vibrant.

God not only expect us to understand His will, He also expects us to understand it alike. This means God expects us to all have the same understanding of His will so we can have unity among us as believers.

Jesus prayed for unity among His followers:

[20] "I do not ask on behalf of these alone, but for those also who believe in Me through

their word; [21] that they may all be one; even as You, Father, are in Me and I in You, that they also may be in Us, so that the world may [a]believe that You sent Me." (John 17:20-21)

The only way to achieve that oneness is for us to understand the Lord's will the same way. This is why the apostle Paul demanded unity among believers:

A. "[10] Now I exhort you, brethren, by the name of our Lord Jesus Christ, that you all [a]agree and that there be no [b]divisions among you, but that you be [c]made complete in the same mind and in the same judgment." (1 Corinthians 1:10)

B. "[2] make my joy complete [a]by being of the same mind, maintaining the same love, united in spirit, intent on one purpose." (Philippians 2:2)

Obviously, Jesus would not pray for unity, nor would Paul demand unity unless unity among all believers was achievable. This means we can and must understand the Scriptures alike. So, why do some still have problems understanding the Scriptures? I believe the reason why people today do not understand the Scriptures is basically three-fold.

First, many make little or no effort to understand the Word of God. They rarely read or study the Bible. Because of this, they are simply spiritually ignorant – they are biblically illiterate! Unfortunately, people who rarely, if ever, read or study the Bible will continue to remain spiritually immature in their knowledge and understanding – and because they are gullible, they will believe anything that sounds good.

Second, some study for the wrong reasons, or with the wrong motives. Some study only when they want to prove themselves right and others wrong. For those who take this approach, their spiritual knowledge and understanding of the Scriptures will remain shallow at best. At worst, those who only study to justify their beliefs run the highest risk of twisting, perverting and misapplying the Scriptures – twisting the Scriptures to make them say something God never intended.

And third, many never grow in their understanding and knowledge of the Scriptures because they simply don't use their God-given common sense. People don't look up words they don't understand; they don't define words in their proper context; or they don't consider everything else God has said on a given subject. This is typical of those who study just for the sake of learning. Unfortunately, they never concern themselves with making an application of God's Word to their own lives.

So, what conclusions can we reach when it comes to understanding the Bible? The only conclusions we can reach are we can and must understand the Bible, and we can and must understand it alike.

The Bible was written so that everyone can learn something; whether children, truth-seekers, new Christians, or those who are spiritually mature.

God's desire is that we not only know and understand the truth, but that we also be obedient to that truth.

"[3] This is good and acceptable in the sight of God our Savior, [4] who desires all men to be saved and to come to the [a]knowledge of the truth. [5] For there is one God, and one mediator also between God and men, the man Crist Jesus," (1 Timothy 2:3-5)

Therefore, the question is not, "Do you understand the Bible?" The question is, "Will you obey what it teaches?"

Notes

Content Summary on Each Bible Book

Genesis	Describes the creation; gives the history of the old world, and of the steps taken by God toward the formation of theocracy.
Exodus	The history of Israel's departure from Egypt; the giving of the law; the tabernacle.
Leviticus	The ceremonial law.
Numbers	The census of the people; the story of the wanderings in the wilderness.
Deuteronomy	The law rehearsed; the death of Moses.
Joshua	The story of the conquest and partition of Canaan.
Judges	The history of the nation from Joshua to Samson.
Ruth	The story of the ancestors of the royal family of Judah.
1 Samuel	The story of the nation during the judgeship of Samuel and the reign of Saul.
2 Samuel	Story of the reign of David.

PATRICK T. BROWN, M.DIV, ED.D

1 and 2 Kings	The books of Kings form only one book in the Hebrew MSS. They contain the history of the nation from David's death and Solomon's accession to the destruction of the kingdom of Judah and the desolation of Jerusalem, with a supplemental notice of the liberation of Jehoiachin from his prison at Babylon, twenty-six years later; they comprehend the whole time of the Israelitish monarchy, exclusive of the reigns of Saul and David.
The Books of Chronicles	The record made by the appointed historiographers of the kingdoms of Judah and Israel; they are the official histories of those kingdoms.
Ezra	The story of the return of the Jews from the Babylonish captivity, and of the rebuilding of the temple.
Nehemiah	A further account of the rebuilding of the temple and city, and of the obstacles encountered and overcome.
Esther	The story of a Jewess who becomes queen of Persia and saves the Jewish people from destruction.
Job	The story of the trials and patience of a holy man of Edom.
Psalms	A collection of sacred poems intended for use in the worship of Jehovah. Chiefly the productions of David.

Proverbs	The wise sayings of Solomon.
Ecclesiastes	A poem respecting the vanity of earthly things.
Solomon's Song	An allegory relating to the church.
Isaiah	Prophecies respecting Christ and his kingdom.
Jeremiah	Prophecies announcing the captivity of Judah, its sufferings, and the final overthrow of its enemies.
Lamentations	The utterance of Jeremiah's sorrow upon the capture of Jerusalem and the destruction of the temple.
Ezekiel	Messages of warning and comfort to the Jews in their captivity.
Daniel	A narrative of some of the occurrences of the captivity, and a series of prophecies concerning Christ.
Hosea	Prophecies relating to Christ and the latter days.
Joel	Prediction of woes upon Judah, and of the favor with which God will receive the penitent people.
Amos	Prediction that Israel and other neighboring nations will be punished by conquerors from the north, and of the fulfillment of the Messiah's kingdom.
Obadiah	Prediction of the desolation of Edom.
Jonah	Prophecies relating to Nineveh.

Micah	Predictions relating to the invasions of Shalmaneser and Sennacherib, the Babylonish captivity, the establishment of a theocratic kingdom in Jerusalem, and the birth of the Messiah in Bethlehem.
Nahum	Prediction of the downfall of Assyria.
Habakkuk	A prediction of the doom of the Chaldeans.
Zephaniah	A prediction of the overthrow of Judah for its idolatry and wickedness.
Haggai	Prophecies concerning the rebuilding of the temple.
Zechariah	Prophecies relating to the rebuilding of the temple and the Messiah.
Malachi	Prophecies relating to the calling of the Gentiles and the coming of Christ.
Gospel of St. Matthew	A brief history of the life of Christ.
Gospel of St. Mark	A brief history of the life of Christ, supplying some incidents omitted by St. Matthew.
Gospel of St. Luke	The history of the life of Christ, with especial reference to his most important acts and discourses.
Gospel of St. John	The life of Christ, giving important discourses not related by the other evangelists.

Acts of the Apostles	The history of the labors of the apostles and of the foundation of the Christian Church.
Epistle to the Romans	A treatise by St. Paul on the doctrine of justification by Christ.
First Epistle to the Corinthians	A letter from St. Paul to the Corinthians, correcting errors into which they had fallen.
Second Epistle to the Corinthians	St. Paul confirms his disciples in their faith and vindicates his own character.
Epistle to the Galatians	St. Paul maintains that we are justified by faith, and not by rites.
Epistle to the Ephesians	A treatise by St. Paul on the power of divine grace.
Epistle to the Philippians	Paul sets forth the beauty of Christian kindness.
Epistle to the Colossians	Paul warns his disciples against errors and exhorts to certain duties.
First Epistle to the Thessalonians	St. Paul exhorts his disciples to continue in the faith and in holy conversation.
Second Epistle to the Thessalonians	St. Paul corrects an error concerning the speedy coming of Christ the second time.
First and Second Epistles to Timothy	St. Paul instructs Timothy in the duty of a pastor and encourages him in the work of the ministry.

Epistle to Titus	Epistle to Titus. St. Paul encourages Titus in the performance of his ministerial duties.
Epistle to Philemon	An appeal to a converted master to receive a converted escaped slave with kindness.
Epistle to Hebrews	St. Paul maintains that Christ is the substance of the ceremonial law.
Epistle of James	A treatise on the efficacy of faith united with good works.
First and Second Epistles of Peter	Exhortations to a Christian life, with various warnings and predictions.
First Epistle of St. John	Respecting the person of our Lord, and an exhortation to Christian love and conduct.
Second Epistle of St. John	St. John warns a converted lady against false teachers.
Third Epistle of St. John	A letter to Gaius, praising him for his hospitality.
Epistle of St. Jude	Warnings against deceivers.
Revelation	The future of the Church foretold.

Notes

Bibliography

Bates, G., & Cosner, L. (2010). *How to Understand the Bible.* Upper Saddle River, NJ: Pearson Merrill Prentice Hall.

Beal, T. (2009) *The Black Church in America: African American Christian Spirituality.* Malden, MA: Blackwell Publishing.

Black, N. (2009). *Biblical literacy: The essential bible stories everyone needs to know.* New York, NY: Harper Collins Publishers.

Mills, G. (2018). *Educational research: Competencies for Analysis and Applications.* New York. Pearson.

Reese, M.P. (2010). *An assessment of bible knowledge of churches of Christ in West Virginia and related variables.* Blue letter Bible

"A Religious Portrait of African Americans. The Pew Forum on Religion & Public Life." Pew Research Center, (2009). https://www.pewforum.org/2009/01/30/a-religious-portrait -of-african-americans/

"*Scripture & Language Statistics 2018*" Wycliffe Global Alliance, (2018). http://www.wycliffe.net/statistics

"*U.S. Religious Landscape Survey: Religious Beliefs and Practices*" Pew Research Center, (2008). https://www.pewforum.org/2008/06/01/u-s-religious-landscape-survey-religious-beliefs-and-practices/

Printed in the United States
By Bookmasters